This book is dedicated to all who find Nature

not an adversary to conquer and destroy, but a storehouse

of infinite knowledge and experience linking man to

all things past and present. They know conserving the natural

environment is essential to our future well being.

GREAT BASIN

THE STORY BEHIND THE SCENERY®

by Michael L. Nicklas

Michael L. Nicklas, raised in the Great Basin along the Wasatch Range, studied forest ecology and wilderness management at the University of Idaho. A career employee of the National Park Service, Mike has served as a park naturalist in Rocky Mountain, Death Valley, and Grand Teton national parks, as well as four years at Great Basin.

Great Basin National Park, *located in eastern Nevada, established in 1986, protects a remnant ice field on Wheeler Peak, ancient bristlecone pine forests, and the decorated galleries of Lehman Caves.*

Front cover: Ancient bristlecone pine at Wheeler Peak, photo by Galen Rowell/Mountain Light. Inside front cover: Stella Lake and Wheeler Peak, photo by Larry Ulrich. Page 1: Bristlecone pine berry, photo by Frank Buckley. Pages 2/3: Stalactites and stalagmites in Lehman Caves, photo by Fred Hirschmann.

Edited by Mary L. Van Camp. Book design by K. C. DenDooven.

Second Printing, 2003

LC 96-75072 ISBN 0-88714-105-6.

*The creation of Great Basin
    National Park is a
unique concept for the Park
    Service, for it preserves not
only the timeless resources found
    within the park's boundaries but also serves to
    represent the vast Great Basin province.*

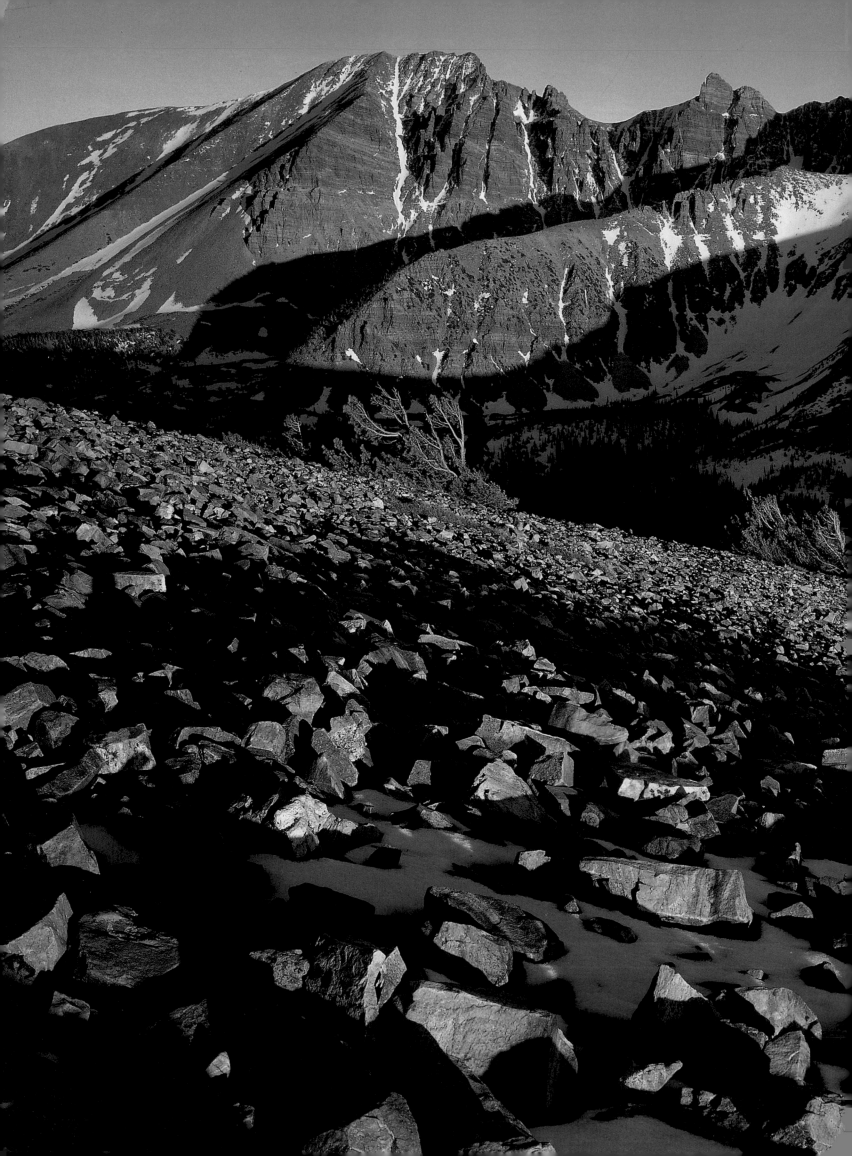

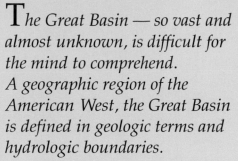

The Great Basin — so vast and almost unknown, is difficult for the mind to comprehend. A geographic region of the American West, the Great Basin is defined in geologic terms and hydrologic boundaries.

Although only a small part of this immense, wild land, Great Basin National Park is undoubtedly the best example of the entire Great Basin region. Its geologic diversity—from windswept playas to mysterious caverns and icy summits— defines the hydrologic boundaries.

Precious water draining from the mountain ranges does not flow into the oceans. Rather, this priceless substance either percolates underground, accumulates in basins to form lakes, or evaporates back into the atmosphere. Water, within this mountain-calloused landscape, creates an incredible diversity of life forms.

Great Basin's only remaining glacier lies sheltered within the national park in the cool shadow of 13,063-foot Wheeler Peak, which also supports bristlecone pines, the oldest living trees on earth. The subterranean wonder of Lehman Caves; the largest limestone arch; endemic species; crystal-clear air and water—all are part of this land of superlatives. Come . . . explore Great Basin!

JEFF GNASS

Sunset bathes the Precambrian, quartzite talus fields and slopes of Jeff Davis Peak and Wheeler Peak.

5

More mountain ranges, all standing in parallel north-south rows, are concentrated in the Great Basin than in all the remainder of North America.

Mountain Islands in a Desert Sea

JEFF GNASS

▲ **R**hyolite cliffs overlook Bog Hot Valley near the Sheldon Antelope Refuge in northwestern Nevada. Rhyolite, a dense-textured, volcanic rock, cooled rapidly at the earth's surface.

The Great Basin is an exciting geologic classroom. It is a place where the rocks seem to "grow wild," where the edges of continents were once located, where land masses slammed together and then were ripped apart. Some of the best evidence to support the theory of plate tectonics is found here. The Great Basin's geologic gradient—from vertical cliffs to flat playas—has influenced plant and animal communities, as well as human history.

ISLAND ARCS

Geologists believe that rocks in northern Nevada are about 2.5 billion years old. That is half the age of Earth itself! At that time, a warm, shallow sea covered this now arid land. Two or three hundred miles to the north of the present park lay an east-west running shoreline (in the vicinity of today's Grouse Creek and Raft River Range of northern Nevada).

About 2 billion years ago, an island arc, part of a small continental plate containing volcanoes, moved north and collided with the shoreline in northern Nevada. Some 10 million years later, another island arc approached from the south and again collided.

We know little of what happened next. There is a large gap in the geologic story, much like reading a good novel only to discover that pages are missing from the book. From about 1.74 billion years ago to about 850 million years ago, entire chapters are missing.

THE BIG RIFT

One chapter that is intact tells of an enormous, north-south trending rift formed in central Nevada about 1.2 billion years ago. The western

JOSEF MUENCH

▲ *The Ruby Mountains, like the Snake Mountains of Great Basin National Park, lie in the heart of the Great Basin, and are made of highly metamorphosed sedimentary rocks—rocks that were changed due to incredible pressures and fiery heat. Later, cracks in these metamorphic rocks were intruded by igneous granites in a molten state forming dikes and sills. Extensional forces in the earth's crust lifted these rocks to create the Ruby Mountains. During the Ice Age, alpine glaciers carved the rocks and mountains to form their present shape.*

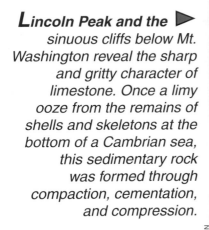

Lincoln Peak and the ▶ *sinuous cliffs below Mt. Washington reveal the sharp and gritty character of limestone. Once a limy ooze from the remains of shells and skeletons at the bottom of a Cambrian sea, this sedimentary rock was formed through compaction, cementation, and compression.*

▲ *The Black Rock Desert in western Nevada exemplifies the flat-floored, desert playas of the Great Basin. Playas, named for the Spanish for beach, are scant reminders of Ice Age lakes that disappeared as the climate dried. Playas may become shallow lakes with frequent precipitation or, after evaporation, glistening white deposits of salt or clay.*

part began to drift off to the northwest, eventually becoming part of what is now Siberia.

The new shoreline was located in today's northern Utah. The warm, shallow sea was underlain at a depth of perhaps 200 yards by a continental shelf, whereupon sediments deposited in the sea came to rest. The layers of sand, silt, and calcium carbonate were later compacted and cemented to form sandstone, shale, and limestone. To the west, beyond the shallow shelf, lay deep ocean. Time passed.

LIFE BEGINS

To the east, what is now Utah was a stark landscape of windswept plains. Sluggish streams crossed the desolate land. The only sounds were from the wind and the moving water—600 million years ago there was no life on the continents. But in the warm, shallow sea were life's beginnings. Preserved in the rocks are fossils, the timekeepers of geology.

Great changes had taken place on the land. A tropical climate now existed with warm temperatures and high humidity. Later, about 150 million years ago, palm, fig, and magnolia trees appeared. The environment was suited for enormous reptiles—the dinosaurs. Their reign lasted from about 225 million years ago to approximately 63 million years ago, when the last dinosaurs became extinct almost overnight.

MOUNTAINS UPLIFTED

Beginning approximately 40 million years ago, the crust of the Great Basin began to pull apart under extensional forces. As it was

JEFF GNASS

stretched in an east-west direction, fractures and faultlines in the thinning crust formed, similar to hairline cracks darting through a piece of glass. Sections of the landscape dropped down to become valleys; other sections rose upward to become mountains.

Mountain ranges of the entire Great Basin province were uplifted to create an undulating landscape containing more than 200 mountain ranges and valley basins in Nevada alone! More mountain ranges, all standing in parallel north-south rows, are concentrated in the Great Basin than in all the remainder of North America.

The Snake Range first began uplifting ▲
perhaps 17 million years ago when a layer of sedimentary rocks began slipping over a core of highly metamorphosed or recrystallized rocks. This slipping occurred along a deep, low-angled faultline called a "decollement" by geologists. As the Great Basin's crust stretched and thinned due to extensional forces caused by the drifting continental plates, enormous blocks slumped down and tilted to form the Basin and Range topography.

9

GLACIERS SCULPT THE MOUNTAINS

Glaciers are one of mountain making's finest chapters. They are the sculptors of the mountains, the artists that carve and shape them—and also tear them down. The glaciers in the Great Basin during the Ice Age were not vast ice sheets that came sweeping out of the north but, rather, occurred at the cool and moist high elevations of the ranges. An alpine glacier is still found on the northeast side of Wheeler Peak. It is the only remaining glacier in the Great Basin—the last link to the Pleistocene Epoch.

Ice pried and plucked the rock formations apart, and the moving glacier then carried the material in a conveyor-belt fashion to its end. The ice scoured the quartzite rock walls on Wheeler Peak and other summits, forming majestic cirques.

When the climate warmed and the glaciers melted, the cirques were not alone as reminders of the Ice Age. Large boulders, small rocks, pebbles, and pulverized rocks carried by the glaciers had been deposited in piles of debris known as moraines.

Meltwater from these glaciers drained into the valleys throughout the Great Basin to form vast lakes. The best known of these Pleistocene lakes are Lake Lahontan in the western part of the province and Lake Bonneville in the east. The Great Salt Lake is what remains of Lake Bonneville after a catastrophic draining and the onset of a drier climate. At Lake Bonneville's greatest volume some 14,500 to 15,000 years ago, its most southwestern reaching arm covered the Snake Valley east of the park.

JOHN DITTLI

▲ *Evidence of passing glaciers can be found on* some boulders and the bedrock in valleys sculpted by the slow-moving ice. Polished rock, complete with scratches and striations as ice moved over the surface, can be located below Pyramid Peak and other major summits where the alpine glaciers carved the landscape.

JOHN P. GEORGE

◄ *Quartzite outcroppings* at Mather Overlook afford a viewing platform for the aspen in autumn's colors. Particles of very hard quartz have been reduced to the size of silt and sand by the labor of ice and water. Wind, over the millennium, carried the silt and sand and deposited the sediments on ancient shorelines or interior drainages. Covered by younger detritus, the sediments are eventually converted to rock.

Wheeler Peak, ▶ standing over 13,000 feet, provides classic examples of the erosional forces of glaciation. Ice pried, plucked, and carried away quartzite from the cool, northeast slopes of the higher reaches in the Snake Range. When the glaciers melted and receded, deep bowls called "cirques" were exposed. Also visible today are the rocky hummocks called moraines. The Wheeler Peak cirque still shelters the only remaining glacier in the Great Basin.

JEFF GNASS

The most recent period of glaciation in the Great Basin ended about 11,000 years ago, and with it faded one of the most breathtaking chapters in the geologic story. But even as the ice melted, the water was working in a different medium—under the ground.

FORMATION OF CAVES

Patiently sculpting Pole Canyon Limestone, water began creating a delicate subterranean wonderland. While water slowly drained into the ground between fractures in the rock, it was also being charged with carbon dioxide, given off by decaying and decomposing organic material of plants and animals. When the solution reached the water table, marble and limestone were dissolved away, creating caverns.

Limestone rock formations make up a large portion of Great Basin National Park, and limestone means cave country. There are numerous explored (and who knows how many undiscovered) caves in the park, but the most famous is Lehman Caves. (See page 38, for more about Lehman Caves.)

Forces in nature create and forces in nature destroy. All are part of this dynamic and changing earth.

SUGGESTED READING

FIERO, BILL. *Geology of the Great Basin.* Reno, Nevada: University of Nevada Press, 1986.

MC PHEE, John. *Basin and Range.* New York, New York: Farrar-Straus-Giroux, 1981.

SCHMIDT, JEREMY. *Lehman Caves.* Salt Lake City, Utah: Lorraine Press, 1987.

The Great Basin Desert

Scanning across the valleys to the distant mountains, one can easily see the delineation between the various plant communities of the Basin and Range country. In dramatic rises in elevation from the olive-silver valley floors to the slate-gray ridgetops, separate and distinct biologic communities reveal their character.

Lowlands and steppes of greasewood, shadscale, or sagebrush communities give way to pinyon pine and juniper woodlands interspersed with stands of quaking aspen and mountain mahogany. Ribbons of riparian habitats including willows and cottonwoods lace the mountainsides. At the mid to upper elevations are the dark green colors of limber pine, Englemann spruce, and bristlecone pine groves of the sub-alpine forest communities. Still higher, above all the other life zones, the alpine community flourishes in a low-lying, procumbent lifestyle where the winds roar.

Subtle differences in the environmental factors juxtapose the various habitats into a quiltwork of biologic communities. Within these sometimes isolated biologic islands of the Great Basin are many stories . . . of the span of geologic history; of species adaptation and migration; and of the survival of ecological communities.

▲ **Greasewood** shrubs can tolerate very salty or alkaline soil conditions. Many dried-up lake beds drain poorly due to the soil's clay content mixed with silt and sand.

PHOTOS BY JEFF GNASS

Moisture from melting ▲
snow or infrequent rain often
pools up due to the soil's clay
content. Many plants have
adapted to this drought-flood
life cycle in salty soils.

◀ **D**ense forests are few in the
Great Basin region. Stands of white fir,
limber pine, and Great Basin bristlecone
pine grow in the cold, windswept
environment of the mountains. During the
Pleistocene these trees lived
in the valleys, but as the climate
warmed and became drier they migrated
to more favorable climates.

▲ **F*ields of lupine decorate the Snake River*** *Plain in Laidlaw Park, Idaho. Lupine, and other members of the pea family, have nodules in their roots that are able to take nitrogen from the air and convert it into plant food, thus enriching the soil with nitrogen. The flowers' color fades after pollination thereby signaling to insects not to waste time searching for nectar.*

▲ **C**onifer trees along Emerald Lake in the Jarbidge Wilderness in northern Nevada may be descendants of a continuous forest that connected the Great Basin to the northern Rocky Mountains. As the climate changed after the Ice Age, the forests and associated species became isolated after migrating up the mountains to more favorable conditions.

◀ **W**inds carry sand particles and sometimes heap the fragments into great dunes in the leeward sides of mountains, or the sand drops out of the vertices of swirling winds caused by canyons or valleys. Occasionally, ancient ripples in the sand are preserved in fossilized dunes.

A river cuts through basalt cliffs of the Owyhee Plateau in southern Idaho marking the northern boundary of the Great Basin. Basaltic cliffs of the Owyhee are a portion of a great mass of dark volcanic rock intrusion called the Snake River batholith covering hundreds of square miles. ▼

Driving up the winding Wheeler Peak Scenic Drive
is like driving
north hundreds of miles.
Elevation becomes latitude.

Communities of Life

PETER FRENCH

▲ *Early winter snow blankets the scene along Lehman Creek. The mountains' winter snowpacks are the storage tanks of water throughout the Great Basin. Born from the winter's melting snow and disappearing a few short miles away in the arid valleys, the streams never directly reach the seas.*

The geology of the Great Basin creates a rich diversity in its flora and fauna. Biological diversity is due largely to the great differences in elevation from valley floors to mountain summits. Basin and Range topography strongly influences the weather patterns and the availability of life-giving water, as moisture-laden storms release widely varying amounts of snow and rain from mountains to valleys.

The plants and animals living here are a tribute to the stubbornness of the evolutionary and natural growth processes of the Great Basin. Isolated by natural barriers of mountain ranges and valley basins, plants and animals must cope with uprooting winds, long periods of killing cold, brief blasts of heat, too little atmosphere, and too much sun—as well as the single most important environmental factor, the scarcity of water. And yet, in spite of (or perhaps because of) what the environment does to make life implausible, biologic diversity abounds in the Great Basin.

Driving up the winding Wheeler Peak Scenic Drive is like driving north hundreds of miles—changes in elevation have the same effect as changes in latitude. The "zonation" of the biologic communities is correlated with elevation (especially here in the Basin and Range country), but is not based on any single factor, unless we regard energy as that factor. Energy in the form of sun-

CHARLES HAIRE

Autumn snows dusting Wheeler Peak signal ▶ *the early arrival of winter on the road to the Wheeler Peak Campground. Typically, long winters grip the land above 10,000 feet from November through June.*

light, thermal radiation, food nutrients, soil, and, of course, moisture. By traveling through the various communities of life, we can investigate some of the fascinating diversity and methods of adaptation organisms have evolved in an environment of such extremes.

VALLEY SAGEBRUSH COMMUNITY

Throughout the lowlands and foothills of the Great Basin, a silvery-green shrub dominates the vistas: sagebrush. Ubiquitous in the Great Basin, sagebrush seems to symbolize the American West. Anyone who has ever smelled its sweet, musky aroma that lingers after a summer rainstorm always remembers the fragrance.

Although sagebrush is unpalatable to livestock and most wildlife, the state of Nevada recognized its importance and declared this hardy schrub the state flower.

PINYON-JUNIPER WOODLAND

As we travel through the sagebrush community to higher elevations, we see a woodland of evergreen trees. After traveling through the shadeless valley floors, the cooler air and dark green foliage of the shrub-like pinyon and juniper trees are welcome.

Pinyon pine usually occurs with one or two species of juniper in the Great Basin. In North America there are eleven species of pinyon, but only the singleleaf pinyon is found in the Great Basin. Pines are cone-bearing evergreen trees with needles appearing in fascicles or groups of two, three, or five, except for singleleaf pinyon pines which have only one needle per fascicle. The pinyon species is grouped with other pines because of its soft wood.

Pinyon pines disperse their large, wingless seeds in a sort of "air-lift." The starchy pinyon pine "nuts" are eaten by many mammals and birds. Associated with the pinyon pine are two species of junipers: Utah and Rocky Mountain. Utah juniper forms an association with pinyon pine but at the lower levels of the woodland, above the sagebrush community, it may be the only species. The trees' round-crowned canopy of coarse foliage produces a berry-like cone that is palatable to fruit-eating birds and mammals.

▲ *An* ocean of sagebrush below the Snake Range. *Sagebrush has solved the problem of acquiring and preserving the desert's most precious substance— water. Sagebrush is the foundation of a unique community that only recently has been appreciated.*

MOUNTAIN-MAHOGANY WOODLAND

Ascending even higher up the slopes of the Snake Range, we encounter patches of mountain-mahogany woodland inhabiting the rocky, windswept inclines and ridges.

▲ *A* **rock squirrel enjoys the tasty and** *nutritious nuts of the thin-shelled, pinyon pine seed. Surprisingly, no tree squirrels are found in the Great Basin.*

CHARLES HAIRE

Curlleaf mountain-mahogany's round canopy rarely exceeds 35 feet in height. Mountain-mahogany occupies diverse environments, mixing with sagebrush and pinyon-juniper communities and also forming distinct ecotones with aspen and conifer groves up to 9,000 feet or more in elevation.

Mountain-mahogany has a fascinating and unusual means of propagating its seeds. The seed is covered with hairs and is about a quarter inch in length with a two- to three-inch hairy, corkscrew-shaped tail. When the dispersed seed becomes wet in a summer rainstorm, the corkscrew-tail becomes turgid and spirals into the soil anchoring the seed for germination the following spring.

CONIFER FOREST COMMUNITY

Traversing the rocky terrain and ascending yet another slope, we enter the mixed conifer forest community. Trees are the pillar of life upon which most of the forest community is dependent.

In September, the cones of the limber pine are ripe with seeds. The undulating flight of the Clark's nutcracker is a common site amongst these trees. Perched on a limber pine, adjacent to a ripe cone, the bird may gulp up to a hundred wingless seeds into its sublingual throat pouch. After flying to a nearby open ridgetop, the nutcracker deposits the seeds in several caches of four or five seeds each. Clark's nutcrackers have exceptional memories, returning to the seed caches throughout the winter months.

JOHN DITTLI

Seed caches that are not retrieved are the germination grounds for seedling limber pine. Limber pine relies solely on the Clark's nutcracker as a seed disperser, and this mutualistic relationship benefits both the tree and the bird.

The winged seeds of Englemann spruce, however, are dispersed by the wind after the cones ripen and dry out. Englemann spruce is a tall and straight tree growing in dense stands. The sharp-needled spruce is often confused with blue spruce, but the latter is not to be found in Great Basin National Park although it does extend as far west as the Deep Creek Range north of the park.

Great Basin flora and fauna are adapted to a seemingly inhospitable and demanding environment. Throughout the Great Basin we expect to find certain organisms in given habitats only to be surprised that some species are absent or that endemic ones exist. Many answers to perplexing questions about the evolution and distribution of the communities of life in the Great Basin are yet to be understood.

SUGGESTED READING

LANNER, RONALD M. *Trees of the Great Basin: A Natural History.* Reno, Nevada: University of Nevada Press, 1984.

RYSER, FRED A. JR. *Birds of the Great Basin: A Natural History.* Reno, Nevada: University of Nevada Press, 1985.

TRIMBLE, STEPHEN. *The Sagebrush Ocean.* Reno, Nevada: University of Nevada Press, 1989.

LANNER, RONALD M. *Made for Each Other: A Symbiosis of Birds and Pines.* Oxford University Press, 1996.

*A***bove treeline, wind dictates the lifestyle of** *the low-lying, procumbent alpine community. On barren, rocky slopes with a short growing season and heavy snowfall, trees take on the stunted* ▼ *growth form called "Krummholz."*

Woodlands of single- ▲
leaf pinyon pine and curlleaf
mountain mahogany
overlook early-morning
fog in the valley. These
drought-resistant, evergreen
gymnosperms and
angiosperms are found in
diverse situations throughout
the Great Basin, and
provide food and shelter for
a host of organisms.

GEORGE WUERTHNER

◀ **P**onderosa pine stands
tall among the shorter pinyon
pine along Lehman Creek. Two
varieties of ponderosa pine are
found in the Basin and Range
province. One variety migrated
into the region from the western
coastal ranges. The other
variety is found in the eastern
ranges of the Great Basin after
migrating from the southern
Rockies after the Pleistocene.

Dense mats of ▷
greenleaf manzanita shrubs impede the passage in Baker Creek. Manzanita with its resinous, highly flammable evergreen leaves is sustained by fire. The dense-wooded shrub produces seeds that are tolerant of high temperatures, are viable for years after dispersal, and germinate after fires pass.

T*he purplish-blue berries of the juniper tree mature in two years. The fleshy berries provide food for birds* such as Townsend's solitaire and Bohemian waxwings. Rodents also eat the berries, and rock squirrels harvest the shaggy bark for lining their nests. While not a true cedar, early settlers referred to junipers as such because ▽ they were reminded of the cedars found on the east and west coasts.

JEFF GNASS

▲ **A** bough of a limber pine frames Jeff
Davis Peak and Wheeler Peak. The sanctuary
of trees and mountains refreshes and inspires.

Curlleaf mountain-mahogany has a dense,
drought-resistant wood that was used to make charcoal
for smelting ores during the mining days of the 1800s.
▼ Charcoal kilns are found throughout the Great Basin.

SALVATORE VASAPOLI

▲ **T**he icy summit of Wheeler Peak towers
above the frigid waters of Teresa Lake. After the
Ice Age, glaciers not only left behind carved
mountains and moraines, but also shallow,
scooped-out basins called tarns like Teresa Lake.
Later, conifers migrated to the upper elevations.

GEORGE WARD

▲ *A sprig of windblown Englemann spruce lies on a* still-life of cones from bristlecone and limber pines and Englemann spruce trees. Seedlings germinated from the accumulated cones huddle from the howling winds creating a micro-environment. Young seedlings trap the windblown dust, helping to establish a sparse soil.

Overleaf: Glacially carved aretes of ▷ quartzite stand guard over the ancient bristlecone pine grove in the Wheeler Peak cirque. Photo by Tom Danielsen.

Bristlecones are perhaps the most intriguing feature of the Great Basin. Walk among the ancient bristlecones... Marvel at their perseverance under adversity.

A Visit With the Ancients

A journey to the park would be incomplete without visiting the ancient bristlecone pines, the quintessence of Great Basin perseverance. Several stands flourish in the remote, upper reaches of the park and throughout the Great Basin. The Wheeler Peak stand is by far the most accessible, and the spectacular amphitheater of the Wheeler Peak cirque is an appropriate and powerful setting for our planet's oldest living trees.

An aura of reverence overcomes visitors in the company of trees that live for millennia. Bristlecone pines stubbornly cling to lofty slopes and windy ridges between 9,000 and 11,500 feet, living for 5,000 years or more. In 1964, a living tree was discovered in the Wheeler Peak grove which contained 4,844 annual growth rings.

In other locations bristlecones attain heights of 60 feet with a diameter of 5 feet. These taller trees grow in environments of relatively abundant moisture and soil and, interestingly, live a much shorter life—1,500 years at most. But the Wheeler Peak grove takes on a more stunted form typical of trees surviving at the upper edges of treeline. At this elevation, winter lasts almost nine months of the year and harsh winds are relentless year-round. The ancient trees seem to thrive in this formidable country of wind and cold on dry, rocky soils.

Stand next to a senior tree and pass your

RICHARD WESTON

◀ *Bristlecone pine cones' dark color retains heat and speeds up the time required for maturity. Upon maturing, the tiny, winged seeds are dispersed by the wind. High elevation bristlecones often grow in clumps, a result of the Clark's nutcrackers caching the seeds.*

JOHN P. GEORGE

The bulk of a 3,000-year-old bristlecone pine ▶ is mostly dead. "Lifelines" of bark still supply precious water from the roots to the needles and food from the needles to the roots. When healthy roots die, the bark sloughs away exposing the resinous wood to the sandblasting effects of the winds.

hand over the smooth wood. Think about the enormity of time. Caress the deep-green needles occurring in groups of five per fascicle. Even the needles are long-lived, surviving up to 40 years by replacing the dead phloem cells that transport the food sugars—characteristic of pines living in high, dry places.

In the early 1970s, the Great Basin bristlecone pine was distinguished as a separate and longer living species than its Rocky Mountain bristlecone pine counterpart. Whorls of the needles grow well down the limbs, with relatively short needles indicating a dry growing season and longer needles indicating wetter times. But the bristlecone's annual growth rings of ancient wood are the greatest of all timekeepers.

A PRICELESS RECORD

The enduring bristlecones are sensitive to periods of severe drought. Years of abundant moisture mean wider than usual growth rings. Rarely is a year missed, making this tree-ring record a priceless tool for science. By "stacking" two- and three-thousand-year-old tree records with other trees that lived and died thousands of years ago, we get a looking-glass view of past climates dating back 9,000 to 10,000 years. The science of dendrochronology allows calibration of the radiocarbon dating curve for precise carbon-dating of organic material. Climatologists, botanists, geologists, and archaeologists reap the benefits of the bristlecone's tree-ring records.

Bristlecone pines that have lived for millennia have mostly exposed wood, the bark growing

◀ *Even in death a bristlecone pine is an invaluable instrument in timekeeping. This approximately 3,000-year-old bristlecone pine died some 300 years ago. The 300 years of records provided by still-living trees added to the 3,000 years this tree lived contributes to a 3,300-year record of the Great Basin climate. Years of abundant moisture are reflected in wide annual tree rings— narrow tree rings mean years of droughts. By adding this 3,300-year record to trees that died centuries ago we get a climatic account reaching nearly to the Ice Age.*

Centuries of ▶ winds have blasted the resinous bristlecone pine with ice and rock fragments carving the long-dead wood. It's not so much that bristlecone pines live such a long time, it's more that the trees take such a long time to die. Dry air, short growing seasons, decay-resistant wood, and infrequent fires may explain why bristlecones live so long, or take so long to die.

in narrow strips of "lifelines." The dense, resinous wood is resistant to decay, leaving the tree's greatest vulnerability in its roots. A parasitic fungus or erosion can cause the roots to dry out and die—the adjacent cells of phloem in the bark then also die and the bark drops away revealing the bare wood. Narrow strips of bark remain on the older trees carrying moisture and nutrients to the still-living needles.

The bristlecone pine's growing season is short. Wind-borne pollen is released from mid-July to August. Maturing cones are blackish-purple in color to retain heat from the sun. The cones mature rapidly in this "passive-solar" system, and open to shed the small-winged seeds from late September to October. At higher elevations, Clark's nutcrackers feed on Bristlecone pine nuts because they are more reliable than limber pine seed crops from year to year. The nutcracker's seed-caching behavior explains why many bristlecone pine trees are in clumps.

Bristlecones are perhaps the most intriguing feature of the Great Basin. They are windows to the past—and perhaps to the future. Recently, scientists measured an increase in the average growth rate of bristlecone pines, perhaps due to increasing amounts of carbon dioxide in our planet's atmosphere. Increasing atmospheric levels of carbon dioxide may be the culprit behind the rise in average temperatures of the atmosphere—global warming.

In the Snake Valley some 15,000 years ago, bristlecone pines lived in rocky outcrops near the shores of ancient Lake Bonneville. Bristlecones and other conifers responded to a warming and drying climate by moving up the mountains to cooler, moister habitats. Acting as barometers for our planet's climate, bristlecones may find insurmountable obstacles to migration if the earth's average atmospheric temperature rises more rapidly than past changes in the climate.

Walk among the ancient bristlecones. Learn from the trees about past climates. Marvel at their perseverance under adversity. Gaze at the dynamic surroundings. Notice a seedling bristlecone and think about time. In geologic terms, the 10,000 year record the bristlecones provide is not a long one. But for humans it is vast, and the ancient trees bond us to living organisms that span a good piece of time. As an anonymous hiker scrawled in the Wheeler Peak summit register: "Take life slow—live like a bristlecone."

Shape and Form

▲ **Centuries of exposure to wind and the** sun's ultraviolet rays have carved and bleached this bristlecone pine tree's trunk.

◄ **Bristlecone pines and limber pines stand** in an open woodland on angular quartzite rocks practically devoid of soil. Seeds from the trees are dispersed by the wind or deposited by birds or small mammals. Seedlings, clustered among the boulders, are sustained by the occasional rain showers or melting snow.

STEPHEN TRIMBLE

GALEN ROWELL/MOUNTAIN LIGHT

▲ **Bristlecones are most vulnerable** in their roots where fungus and erosion can cause eventual death.

Sunrise warms a splintered ▷ fragment of bristlecone pine and the east face of Wheeler Peak.

JOHN DITTLI

◁ **Like a** banner, an ancient bristlecone endures among blocks of quartzite boulders at the upper limits of its range. These remarkable trees can be found clinging precariously to rocky ridges above 11,000 feet.

31

Gone were the long, gray winter of the Ice Ages;
the climate was warming and drying
forcing the people of the Great Basin
to develop a broader food-gathering lifestyle.

Those Who Came Before . . .

Much of what we know today about the prehistoric people of the Great Basin comes from excavations of open sites, caves, and rock shelters. The dry climate of this arid land has preserved cultural resources remarkably well.

PALEO-INDIANS

Within the Great Basin, some of the earliest well-dated sites are found from the Paleo-Indian Period, roughly 12,000 B.C. to 9000 B.C. Primarily big game hunters, the Paleo-Indians traveled in small and very mobile groups following and hunting herds of the now-extinct megafauna including mammoth, bison, camel, and horse.

The Paleo-Indians' surroundings rapidly changed. Gone were the long, gray winters of the Ice Ages—the climate was warming and drying forcing the peoples of the Great Basin to develop a broader food-gathering lifestyle.

Seed-grinding implements of millingstones and manos for processing hard-shelled grass seeds reflect consumption of a wider range of food products found in sites from the Great Basin Desert Archaic Period (9000 B.C. to A.D. 400). People became more season-oriented, living in the lowlands in the winters, then moving to the uplands during the summers.

FREMONT CULTURE

The distinctive Fremont culture represented a diversified people who settled in the Great Basin region beginning about A.D. 500 and raised corn for nearly 800 years until vanishing in the 14th century, possibly due to a prolonged drought. In addition to their horticultural lifestyle, the people were gatherers and hunters,

DAVID CAVAGNARO

▲ **American Indians of the Great Basin developed** *a dependency upon the singleleaf pinyon pine nut crop. The native peoples kept track of the cycles and timed their harvests accordingly.*

using roots and seeds for food, and plant fibers to make ropes, shoes, clothing, and baskets. To supplement their diet, the Fremont fashioned bows and arrows for hunting—some of which have been dated to approximately A.D. 500 (earlier than the weapon was used by eastern Indians). They manufactured pottery, using these rough ceramics for bowls and storing vessels for grains and water. They also created their own unique rock art, including pictographs (paintings) and petroglyphs (etchings), examples of which can still be seen.

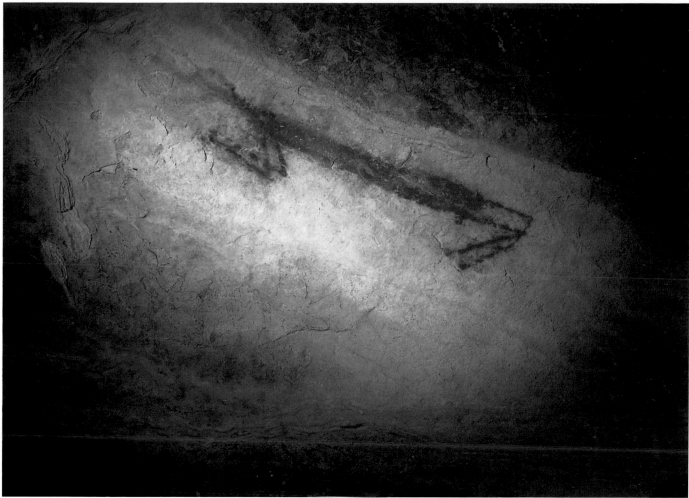

▲ **R**ock art is an abundant cultural resource found throughout the Great Basin. Rock art includes *two styles—pictographs and petroglyphs. Pictographs, like this cricket figure, are designs drawn on rocks with dry pigments. Petroglyphs are designs that are cut, scratched, or pecked into the surfaces of cliffs or boulders. While rock art is not writing, it is symbolic meanings and concepts communicated through images. We will never fully understand the ideology, but by visiting a rock art site we begin to sense the relationship the native peoples had between ceremony, art, and the natural world.*

Living communally in rectangular, adobe pit lodges, the Fremont people dwelt mostly in present-day Utah; however, Fremont-style rock art and cultural objects are found throughout Great Basin National Park, and excellent sites are still being discovered.

SHOSHONE AND PAIUTE

By the 14th century, and after the disappearance of the Fremont culture, the Numic-speaking peoples entered the Great Basin. Their modern-day descendants are the Western Shoshone and the Southern and Northern Paiute peoples. These groups, though distinct, spoke related languages and had similar lifestyles.

The native people of the Great Basin knew the land intimately and understood the natural cycles. Small family groups hunted and gathered, patterning their lives to take advantage of the diverse and abundant resources. The land pro-

vided all their nutritional needs as well as material goods for clothing and shelter. They hunted small and large game, such as jackrabbits and antelope, gathered pine nuts and berries, and dug roots and tubers. Where geography allowed, some fished and farmed small plots. Their knowledge of plant properties allowed them to make medicines as well, treating everything from colds to heart problems to small pox with the bark, roots, and leaves of numerous plants. They were resilient, flexible, and adaptable people.

Fall was a season of gathering and celebration, when small, dispersed kin groups came together for the harvesting of pinyon nuts, accompanied by communal rabbit and antelope drives. This was a time for reunions and marriages. It was a season of plenty. During the winter, families grouped together, telling stories in the evenings and living off their stores gathered in summer and fall.

▲ *Mountain ranges provided reliable water and* *food sources for American Indians in the Great Basin.* *Settlements were transitory and temporarily occupied by* *extended family groups. The Great Basin populations* *were ever on the move, shifting from one food gathering* *place to another. Families cooperated together in* *subsistence endeavors, particularly in the autumn, such* *as harvesting crops of pinyon pine nuts or participating in* *rabbit and antelope drives. Families enjoyed a time of* *heightened ceremonial and recreational activities during* *these communal events.*

▲ *Yellow flowers of the many-spined prickly* *pear bloom in late spring and early summer. Prickly* *pear, like many Great Basin inhabitants, has solved* *the problem of acquiring water. The waxy coating* *on the stem of the drought-tolerant plant prevents* *loss of moisture through evaporation. American* *Indians and settlers learned that the fruit makes a* *tasty treat and, in emergencies, the stem of the* *prickly pear could be used as a source of water.*

At one time at least seven villages were in the Snake Valley, with perhaps 1,000 people. These basin dwellers constructed semi-permanent, conical-shaped houses supported by pole frames and covered with desert brush to serve as shelters during the cold months. Earth and willow sweathouses were constructed, and caves and rock shelters also provided modest housing.

THE EXPLORERS

By 1750, Euro-Americans had explored much of the New World—except for the heart of the American West, the Great Basin. Spain had

established several missions along the California coast and needed to supply and protect these outposts.

In 1776, Franciscan Fathers Escalante and Dominguez left Santa Fe searching for another passageway to the West Coast. The Escalante-Dominguez expedition explored the eastern portions of the Great Basin near Milford and Beaver, and perhaps came as close as 90 miles to present-day Great Basin National Park.

Competing fur companies operating on the American frontier spurred the next Euro-American penetration of the Great Basin. Jedediah Smith, a partner in the Rocky Mountain Fur Company, headed south in 1826 through Utah searching for more sources of beaver pelts. Eventually his expedition of 15 men reached southern California only to be detained by the

Mexican authorities. Smith and two of his men escaped the Mexicans, crossed the Sierra Nevada and traveled east across the midsection of the Great Basin.

Smith's desperate journey was filled with hardships. Stumbling over Connor's Pass to the west of the present-day park, Smith and his men then crossed Sacramento Pass returning to the Rocky Mountains, becoming the first Euro-Americans to traverse the Great Basin.

Almost 20 years later, Congress commissioned U.S. Army Captain John C. Fremont to explore the unknown province. Fremont's expedition of 1843-44 crisscrossed the province and reported the internally draining basin as "truly a great basin." Fremont's greatest contribution to the opening of the West was his work in the Great Basin. His document was the first to explain the many secrets of this land of "contents almost unknown."

SETTLERS

Colonization began in 1847 in the Salt Lake Valley with the arrival of Mormon pioneers

Autumn colors decorate Wheeler Peak at sunrise. Jedediah Smith was the first white American to traverse the Great Basin in 1827. Later, Mormon settlers made the first documented ascent of Wheeler Peak in 1855. Western Shoshone referred to the peak as "Pe-up" meaning "big mountain." The mountain is named for Lt. George Wheeler, leader of an 1869 government survey expedition.

under the leadership of Brigham Young. By the mid-1850s, the Mormons had expanded to 40 settlements in the eastern Great Basin.

In 1855, Brigham Young sent a group of elders to establish a mission and plant crops in the "Grease Wood Valley" (the Snake Valley). The missionaries established a site near present-day Garrison, Utah. Another expedition, the White Mountain Expedition, in 1858 explored the Snake Range and other ranges while establishing a mission near present-day Panaca, Nevada.

The discovery of gold in California in 1848 suddenly created a need to link the West Coast with the rest of the country. Government route and mapping surveys completed scientific ex-

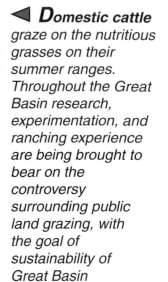

Domestic cattle graze on the nutritious grasses on their summer ranges. Throughout the Great Basin research, experimentation, and ranching experience are being brought to bear on the controversy surrounding public land grazing, with the goal of sustainability of Great Basin ecosystems.

GAIL BANDINI

ploation and military reconnaissance in the late 1850s and 1860s. Lt. George Wheeler, for whom Wheeler Peak is named, led a U.S. Army Corps of Engineers expedition in 1869 and made detailed observations of the Snake Range. A government geodetic survey constructed a triangulation station on Wheeler Peak's summit in 1878.

MINERS

Miners turned their attention to the desolate mountains and, in 1859, mining operations first began in White Pine County. The exciting discovery of gold on the northwestern slopes of the Snake Range caused the town of Osceola to mushroom to a population of 5,000.

The boomtowns lured professionals in all the other businesses and services that accompanied a rapidly growing mining settlement: carpenters, blacksmiths, merchants, prostitutes, bankers, and ranchers. Times were heady and fast-paced during Nevada's exciting mining booms.

The age-old Great Basin problem of lack of

water hampered large-scale mining operations. By 1890, the Osceola Gravel Mining Company had constructed two aqueducts (one 18 miles, and 16 miles) at the cost of over $180,000 to divert water to the placer mining operation. The gamble did not pay off, and in 1901 the Osceola Ditch closed due to dry winters, leaky wooden flumes, water theft, and water rights disputes.

RANCHERS

Absalom S. Lehman settled in the Snake Valley in 1869 and established a ranch on

JOHN DITTLI

Throughout the park and the Great Basin visitors can still discover cabins used by prospectors in the 1800s. Old structures and mines are dangerously unstable and should never be entered.

Lehman Creek. Before his 1885 discovery of the caverns named for him, Lehman, a successful entrepreneur, provided food stuffs such as vegetables, fruit, meat, and dairy products for the miners and prospectors.

Over the following years several other ranchers settled in the area. Cattle were introduced to the Snake Range, grazing in the lush meadows during the late springs and early summers. Sheep were also introduced, and many Basque sheepherders immigrated to the area from the Pyrennees Mountains of Europe. Lonely sheepherders recorded dates and carved colorful drawings on aspen trees that can still be found.

Ranching is an integral part of Great Basin history. The law that created the park permitted grazing to remain unless grazing permits were donated back to the park. In 1999, cattle grazing was retired after a mutual understanding by ranchers, conservations groups, and the park.

SUGGESTED READING

CLINE, GLORIA GRIFFEN. *Exploring the Great Basin.* Reno, Nevada: University of Nevada Press, 1988.

MADSEN, DAVID. *Exploring the Fremont.* Salt Lake City: Utah Museum of Natural History, 1989.

STRONG, EMORY. *Stone Age in the Great Basin.* Portland, Oregon: Binford and Mort, 1969.

CRUM, STEPHEN. *The Road on Which We Came.* University of Nevada Press, 1996.

ED COOPER

▲ **G**old was discovered on the northwest slopes of the Snake Range in the 1870s, but lack of water made large-scale mining operations impossible. Two Osceola Ditches diverted water 18 miles to the mining operation. The Ditches were abandoned in 1901 after years of drought, leaky flumes, water theft, and rights disputes. Portions of the Osceola Ditch remain today.

JEFF GNASS

◀ **A**spen bark became a surface for early 20th century "graffiti artists" who carved names, dates, and figures on the young aspen trees. Their work still exists on the trees' bark, but today's visitors are more sensitive to defacing natural resources and such actions are prohibited in the national park.

Lehman Caves

Limestone rocks were dissolved away by acidic groundwater during the Pleistocene Epoch to form caverns at the water table level. When the water table dropped at the end of the Ice Age, the chamber became filled with air. Carbonic acid percolating down to the cavern releases carbon dioxide and the mineral calcite is deposited in weird yet fascinating formations called speleothems.

Lehman Caves, known about for centuries by local tribes and "discovered" by Absolom Lehman in 1885, can be enjoyed year-round on a leisurely paced tour with a park naturalist. A visit through the caverns becomes a subterranean adventure into a cool, damp world of darkness and overpowering silence. . . a world that time seems to have forgotten. Crystalline formations of calcite range from delicate helictites to stately stalactites, stalagmites, and columns. Symmetrical shields, formations rarely found in other caverns, abound in Lehman Caves and raise perplexing questions about their origin.

Diversity, a Great Basin trait, is represented in the mysterious underground chambers of Lehman Caves.

Calm pools of water remaining in Lehman ▲ Caves act as mirrors for speleothems rendering reflections and reality indistinguishable. Depth of the pools is dependent upon the annual precipitation and melting snow.

TOM BEAN

◀ **F**ingerlike helictites that appear to defy gravity develop from a stalactite. The central tube of this stalactite has become plugged forcing water, under capillary action, to the surface generating twisted curls of calcite.

*"**T**he Parachute," a shield formation named for its apparent image, has come to symbolize Lehman Caves. Shields (calcite formations that extend from a crack in the cave wall), although rather uncommon cave formations, are abundant in Lehman Caves. Calcium carbonate is deposited along the edges of two parallel plates radiating from the crack when water, under hydrostatic pressure and capillary action, is forced through the fissure. Excess solution completes the decoration of the shield by forming drapery, stalactites, or columns on the lower portion of the plates. Permits are required to enter wild caves within the national park.*

ED COOPER

***A**dventurous cavers pursue the thrill ▷ of exploring caves in a wild state. Armed with hard hats for protection, headlamps to probe the blackness, and gloves to protect the delicate speleothems from humans' damaging bodily oils, cavers delight in the pursuit of exploring the labyrinths of caves. Wilderness caving should only be done by the most prepared and experienced cavers to protect the unique ecosystems of caves and to ensure the cavers' safety.*

FRED HIRSCHMANN

FRED HIRSCHMANN

◄ **Frescoes of**
flowstone draperies decorate the narrow passageways. Thin films of carbonic acid solution flowing down the cave wall and over other decorations releases carbon dioxide depositing calcite formations of flowstone.

Drapery, ▶
resembling a hanging screen of calcite, decorates the cave in sinuous curves. Carbonic acid solution making its way into the cavern moves down the sloped ceiling and walls leaving behind a wandering trail of calcite to form drapery.

TOM BEAN

▲ **Cave ornaments are a product**
of water and time. Stalactites may take 100 years to grow one inch!

Backlighting illuminates the variety of colors in ▶
translucent cave formations. Bands of coloring are the result of trace amounts of minerals such as iron and manganese oxides.

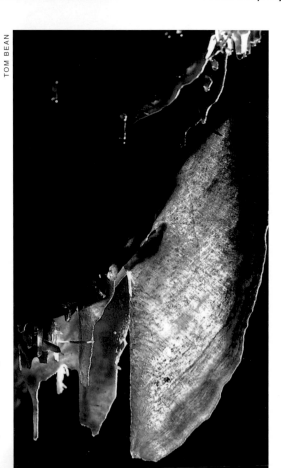

TOM BEAN

ED COOPER

*The National Park Service has a mandate to
protect all the ecosystems represented in our country...
Great Basin National Park helps complete
the collection of our country's special ecosystems.*

Great Basin Today

Absalom Lehman introduced tourism to eastern Nevada by sharing with locals and travelers the wonders of Lehman Caves. The cave was protected on January 24, 1922, when President Warren G. Harding established by presidential proclamation Lehman Caves National Monument. The monument was administered by the U.S. Forest Service until the cave was turned over to the National Park Service in 1933.

The path leading toward the establishment of Great Basin National Park was long and difficult. Proposals first surfaced in 1924 and resurfaced in June 1955, at a meeting of the White Pine County Chamber of Commerce and Mines.

Rediscovery of the glacier on the flank of Wheeler Peak gave additional strength to the proposal for a national park. As word spread about the unique geologic and biologic diversity of the area, support came from national conservation organizations.

Finally, the last, and this time successful, campaign to establish Great Basin National Park began in 1985. What started as a wilderness proposal for National Forest areas in Nevada was

(text continues on page 48)

GALEN ROWELL/MOUNTAIN LIGHT

▲ **National Park Service Director**
*William P. Mott speaking at the park's
dedication on August 15, 1987.*

A *hiker negotiates a tricky mountain stream* ▶
*crossing. Water, in varying amounts and forms within
the Great Basin, is the most precious of resources—
the asset that imparts value to the landscape.*

PATRICK CONE

JOHN DITTLI

42

MIKEL CONRAD

▲ **A**n individual bristlecone pine seedling, some 50 years young, begins its long journey through life. The next generation of the longest-living organisms carries into the future the genetic make-up that evolved to over the past millennium.

GALEN ROWELL/MOUNTAIN LIGHT

▲ **G**reat Basin bristlecone pines endure in the dramatic cirque on Wheeler Peak that is appropriate for the earth's most ancient beings.

◀ **W**ild horses race over the high desert plains of Stone Cabin Valley in the south central part of the Great Basin. Domestic livestock have escaped and live in a feral state in a land of open range and few fences.

43

Winter brings abundant snow to the park's upper elevations. Skiers are rewarded for their long approaches with wilderness skiing adventures.

MIKE NICKLAS

MIKE NICKLAS

Climbers challenge their skills by pioneering new routes, yet should be prepared to conduct self-rescue in the event of an accident.

Park naturalists conduct guided walks to the Wheeler Peak bristlecone pine grove during the summer months, describing the natural history of the ancient trees on the three-mile hike.

MIKEL CONRAD

FRANK S. BALTHIS

Horseback riding for recreation or working livestock remains an efficient mode of travel in the park.

WINDY CANYON

BLUE CANYON

BLUE RIDGE

Osceola Ditch

Mill Creek

BURNT MILL CANYON

487

488

Baker

Buck Mountain
10972ft
3344m

Bald Mountain
11562ft
3524m

Lehman Creek

Lower Lehman
Creek
7300ft
2225m

Lehman Creek

Wheeler Peak
9886ft
3013m

Upper Lehman Creek
7752ft
2362m

Lehman Caves

Visitor Center
6825ft
2080m

Stella
Lake

Teresa
Lake

Brown Lake

GREAT BASIN

SNAKE

Moraine

Glacier   Jeff Davis
12771ft
3893m

Wheeler Peak
13063ft
3982m

Baker Creek
7530ft
2295m

Baker Peak
12298ft
3748m

12305ft
3751m

Baker Creek

POLE CANYON

CAN YOUNG CANYON

KIOUS BASIN

CANYON

Mahogany Spring

Baker Lake

South Fork

Timber Creek

11456ft
3492m

NATIONAL PARK

YOUNG

Clay Spring

11540ft
3517m

Pyramid Peak
11926ft
3635m

10842ft
3305m

10249ft
3142m

HORSE HAVEN

Spring Creek

WILLIAMS CANYON

Johnson Lake

Dead
Lake

11775ft
3589m

GRANITE
BASIN

DRY CANYON

8250ft
2515m

Shoshone

Mt Washington
11658ft
3553m

RANGE

Snake Creek
7680ft
2340m

Snake Creek

BOX CANYON

POLE

CANYON

10885ft
3318m

North

Fork

Lincoln Peak
11597ft
3535m

11001ft
3353m

South Fork

11532ft
3515m

LINCOLN CANYON

HIGHLAND

RIDGE

Johns Wash

Mustang
Spring

11016ft
3357m

DECATHON

Granite Peak
11218ft
3419m

Lexington Arch

ARCH CANYON

10699ft
3261m

CANYON

80

80

93

Salt Lake City

UTAH
NEVADA

15

50

Great
Basin
N.P.

93

15

ARIZONA

Las Vegas

15

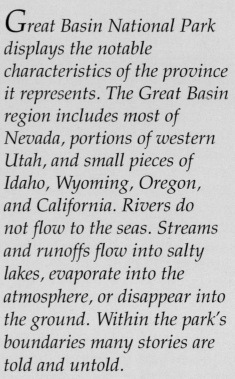

Great Basin National Park displays the notable characteristics of the province it represents. The Great Basin region includes most of Nevada, portions of western Utah, and small pieces of Idaho, Wyoming, Oregon, and California. Rivers do not flow to the seas. Streams and runoffs flow into salty lakes, evaporate into the atmosphere, or disappear into the ground. Within the park's boundaries many stories are told and untold.

The park's geologic history helps explain the stories of plate tectonics and the Great Basin's structural geology. Accounts of forces creating and destroying, and stories of changing landscapes are relayed within the park. The park is alive with narratives about the mountains and valleys, glaciers and caverns, climates and organisms, migration and adaptation, history and prehistory, and the Great Basin's never-ending story—change and time.

Intricate stalactites outline fissures in the marbly, limestone ceiling of the Grand Palace in Lehman Caves. Ever slowly, the cave is being filled with wondrous formations in a reversal of the chemical processes that created the caverns.

amended to include the establishment of the park. President Ronald Reagan signed the Great Basin National Park Act on October 27, 1986—some 60 years after the first efforts to create a national park.

Although Death Valley National Park includes portions of the Great Basin region, the biological and geological diversity of this vast region was not represented in the park system until 1986. The formation of Great Basin National Park helps complete the collection of our country's special ecosystems—it is one of the jewels that was missing in the crown. But it is also a unique concept in the park system, for it protects and preserves an area that is representative of the much greater Basin and Range country of the American West.

Modern visitors make a considerable commitment just getting to the park to satisfy their curiosity about an unexplored land. We travel great distances to wonder at mysterious caverns, to marvel at the astonishing bristlecone pines, to breathe deeply, and escape the crowded places.

As individuals, we are charged by the energy of the fresh winds that swirl above the playas, race over the alpine rocks and through the ancient trees. As a nation, we shall learn from the Great Basin about geologic history, past climates, evolution, and biological diversity. By visiting and studying the spectacular Great Basin, we learn about our local and worldwide environments—and we learn about ourselves.

DAVID CAVAGNARO

Bristlecone pines symbolize the breathtaking vastness of the basins and the massiveness of the mountain ranges.

KC Publications has been the leading publisher of colorful, interpretive books about National Park areas, public lands, Indian lands, and related subjects for over 40 years. We have 6 active series—over 135 titles—with Translation Packages in up to 8 languages for over half the areas we cover. Write, call, or visit our web site for our full-color catalog.

Our series are:

The Story Behind the Scenery® – Compelling stories of over 65 National Park areas and similar Public Land areas. Some with Translation Packages.

in pictures... The Continuing Story® – A companion, pictorially oriented, series on America's National Parks. All titles have Translation Packages.

For Young Adventurers™ – Dedicated to young seekers and keepers of all things wild and sacred. Explore America's Heritage from A to Z.

Voyage of Discovery® – Exploration of the expansion of the western United States.

Indian Culture and the Southwest – All about Native Americans, past and present.

Calendars – For National Parks in dramatic full color, and a companion Color Your Own series, with crayons.

To receive our full-color catalog featuring over 135 titles—Books, Calendars, Screen Scenes, Videos, Audio Tapes, and other related specialty products:

Call (800-626-9673), fax (702-433-3420), write to the address below, Or visit our web site at www.kcpublications.com

Published by KC Publications, 3245 E. Patrick Ln., Suite A, Las Vegas, NV 89120.

***I**nside back cover:* Wilderness sanctuaries arouse a sense of belonging in all creatures. Artwork by Roy Purcell.

***B**ack cover:* Lexington Arch, a rare, 75-foot-high limestone arch, is located in a remote valley of the park. Photo by John P. George.

Created, Designed, and Published in the U.S.A.
Printed by Tien Wah Press (Pte.) Ltd, Singapore
Pre-Press by United Graphic Pte. Ltd